PET OWNER'S GUIDE TO THE
SNAKE

Fred Nind BVM&S MRCVS

RINGPRESS

ABOUT THE AUTHOR

Fred Nind BVM&S MRCVS (left) is a veterinary surgeon who ran his own practice in Edinburgh for 25 years. He has a special interest in treating the more unusual species kept as pets and has a particular fondness for reptiles. He is a past president of the Scottish Herpetological Society and has taken part in congresses on the veterinary care of reptiles from Florida to the Netherlands.

PHOTOGRAPHY
Fred Holmes.

**Published by Ringpress Books,
A Division of INTERPET LTD
Vincent Lane, Dorking, Surrey RH4 3YX**

First published 2002
©2002 Ringpress Books Limited. All rights reserved

Design: Rob Benson

ISBN 1 86054 134 8

Printed and bound in Hong Kong through Printworks International Ltd.

CONTENTS

1

INTRODUCING THE SNAKE   6

Snake ancestors; Snake features (Eyes; Hearing; Heat-sensing pits; Sense of smell; Dentition; Venom; Catching food; Snake anatomy; Body temperature; Urinary system); Owning a snake; Health insurance; Human health concerns (Salmonella; Bites); Life expectancy; Finding out more.

2

SNAKE SPECIES   18

The best choices; (Royal Python; Garter Snake; Milk Snake; King Snake; Burmese Python; Boa constrictor; Corn Snake) Snakes to avoid (Venomous Species; Bad-tempered species; Giant snakes; CITES-listed species).

3

BUYING A SNAKE   27

Snakes for sale (Wild-caught; Captive-farmed; Captive-bred); Signs of good health; Questions to ask; Private sale; Reptile shops; Mail order; Reptile rescues; Age to buy; Sexing; The home-coming.

4

SETTING UP HOME   33

Types of accommodation; Ventilation; Heating; Heat gradients; Lighting; Security; Decor; Introducing plants; Climbing features; Water elements; Substrates (Newspaper; Artificial turf; Bark chips; Gravel, pebbles and sand; Corn kernels); Cleaning.

CARING FOR YOUR SNAKE 47

The snake diet; Water; Vitamin and mineral supplements; Shedding; Keeping the habitat clean; Temporary accommodation; Handling.

BREEDING SNAKES 57

General considerations; Colour morphs; Species and high-breds; Conditioning for breeding; Changing seasons; Egg-layers and live-bearers; Egg incubation; Incubation rules; The home-made incubator; Hatching; Dystochia; Raising the offspring.

HEALTH CARE 69

Snake-friendly vets; Health records; Quarantine; Shedding; Nose-rubbing; Lack of appetite; Tips to tempt a reluctant feeder; Mouth rot; Mites; Internal parasites; Viruses; Respiratory disease; Burns; Thiamine deficiency; Swollen eyes; Nursing care.

1 Introducing The Snake

Snakes are emotive animals. You either love them or hate them. Many people have never touched one, and those that have are often surprised to discover that they are warm, dry and smooth, when they had expected them to be cold, wet and slimy.

Snakes are completely covered in scales, which are often brilliantly coloured. Reds, yellows, greens, blues and purples can all be found, often on the same snake.

Some of the seemingly duller-coloured scales are actually iridescent and will flash every colour of the rainbow as the sun catches them.

SNAKE ANCESTORS

As a group, snakes are all long, thin vertebrates that have no limbs. It is thought that they originally developed from a legless lizard ancestor. Perhaps they evolved in this way to aid rapid

Texas Rat Snake: The snake has no limbs, but it can move at a formidable pace.

Spurs, the vestiges of limbs, can be seen in some species.

movement through thick vegetation or for burrowing through loose soil or sand.

Their ancestors can be traced back to the Cretaceous Period (from 100 million to 150 million years ago), which means that they were around to see the end of the dinosaurs – a long pedigree.

In some species, such as the Boa Constrictor, the last tiny vestiges of the hind legs can be seen as small spurs either side of the vent. These spurs still have a purpose – as we will see later. It has nothing to do with the original purpose of hind legs.

Nevertheless, snakes can get around pretty quickly. They have been clocked at 11 kph (7 mph), which is faster than most people can run. Strikes against a potential food target or an enemy can be even faster, with the strike, bite

and withdraw being completed before you even know that it has started.

In the course of their evolution, snakes have also lost their movable eyelids and their external ears.

At first you might pity snakes for what they have lost but, in fact, they are a very successful group of species, superbly adapted to their role in life.

SNAKE FEATURES

EYES

Most snakes have good eyesight, with organs that work in much the same way as human eyes.

One difference is that they lack movable eyelids. The top and bottom lids are fused together and have become transparent. The skin over these lids sheds at the same time as the snake sheds the rest of its skin. One of the tasks of the diligent reptile keeper is to check each sloughed skin to make sure that the eye caps have come off properly.

Tears bathe the eye itself, underneath the lids, in the same way that they do in our eyes. After they have done their job, these tears will drain away into the mouth through a tiny tube which is called the tear duct.

Red Tail Boa: The top and bottom eyelids are fused together, and are transparent.

Snakes cannot cry, so infections of the front of the eye, or excessive production of tears over and above what can be drained away down the tear duct, will cause problems (see Chapter Seven).

HEARING

During their evolution, snakes have lost the external ears that their ancestors had, together with any internal hearing apparatus.

However, snakes still seem to be able to appreciate sound. This may be by feeling vibrations through the skin.

Or they may be able to detect movement of the ground – rather like the cowboys in films who can tell when the train is coming by pressing their ear to the railway track.

HEAT-SENSING PITS

Some snake species, such as the pythons, possess pits round the snout that are acutely sensitive to heat.

They are said to be able to detect changes of 0.1 degrees C (0.2 degrees F), which is a useful feature when trying to identify a prey animal in an underground tunnel.

The dead, frozen, thawed and then warmed-up rodent that we offer to such a snake in a vivarium is most unlikely to be at that animal's normal, live, body temperature. This could well be one of the reasons why we sometimes have difficulty in persuading our reptile charges to eat.

SENSE OF SMELL

Snakes use their tongues to smell. A healthy snake that is curious about its environment will flick its forked tongue out of its mouth every few seconds to 'taste' the air.

Molecules in the air are trapped on the tongue, which is then withdrawn into the mouth. The tongue is then pushed into two specialised pits on the roof of the mouth, called the 'Jacobson's organs', which can analyse the 'smell'.

At rest, the tongue resides in a sheath on the floor of the snake's mouth.

THE JAW

The lower jaw of the snake is unusual in that the bones that form on each side are not firmly joined to each other in the middle. Instead they are separated by an elastic membrane. Hence there is a popular myth that snakes can dislocate their jaws.

In fact, the snake merely parts the two sides of the lower jaw when eating in order to make a bigger mouth opening to get round the prey. The snake will also 'walk' the two sides of the jaw, in turn, along the creature that it is eating, to help move it into its mouth.

DENTITION

Each jaw is lined with sharp, backwards-projecting teeth. The snake does not chew its food. The teeth are used, instead, to grip the prey and to act like the barbs on fishhooks to prevent the animal slipping back out of the mouth once it has started to be eaten.

Red Sided Garter Snake: A forked tongue is flicked from the mouth to 'taste the air'.

A snake may take as long as 30 minutes to swallow a big meal.

Damaged or lost teeth are replaced by new ones, which grow nearby.

VENOM

Venomous snakes have specialised teeth in the upper jaw. These may be located at the back of the mouth, in rear-fanged snakes, or at the front.

The most dangerous snakes for man have their venom teeth at the front. These teeth are associated with special glands that produce the toxin. As the snake bites, the venom is guided down the fang, either in a groove or a tube within the structure of the tooth.

Different poisonous snakes produce venoms with different effects. Some paralyse the prey, others affect the blood-clotting system and others are tissue-destructive. It may take days for the poisoned animal to die and the snake will patiently follow it on that last journey.

Snakes may take anything up to half an hour to swallow a big meal. During this time the prey animal may block most of the mouth. The entrance to the snake's airway is well forward on the floor of the mouth, and is much more mobile than in a human throat. This helps the snake to breathe during the prolonged swallowing process.

CATCHING FOOD

Snakes have different ways of catching food. Some lie in wait to ambush passing prey, while others are active hunters.

The constrictors do not actually squeeze their prey to death. They form coils round their victim and

tighten them only when the prey breathes out. The actual pressure is quite mild. It is only enough to stop the prey drawing in more air. Death is by suffocation.

Other snakes kill by injecting venom or eating the prey alive.

SNAKE ANATOMY

Being a long and thin animal, the internal organs of the snake also have to be long and thin. They are aligned along the body, in order, and can be found by measuring from the nose to the vent.

Mountain King Snake: The snake is long and thin, and therefore it follows that the internal organs must be of a similar size and shape.

For example, the heart is usually found about one-third of the way along the snake's body and can often be seen beating if you look carefully on the under-surface. Most snakes have only one lung.

At the rear end is the cloaca, a common opening connecting the gastrointestinal tract, the urinary system and the reproductive system, to the outside of the body.

This appears as a slit across the underside of the snake. The change in the scale pattern at this point may help you to recognise it.

BODY TEMPERATURE
Snakes are not really cold-blooded. The temperature of the blood in a snake basking under a nice warm spotlight will be nearly the same as yours.

It is not even true to say that snakes cannot control their body temperature. They can. But they do not do it by burning food energy as you and I do.

A snake will control its temperature by moving to different environments at different temperatures, and then cooling or warming up to the ambient temperature. This has the big advantage of using less energy. A snake's calorie needs are a fraction of those of a dog or cat of

equivalent size, and it can go many months without eating. However the metabolic processes such as digestion or immunity will not work properly at the wrong temperature.

It is therefore important for the snake to be able to stay in its POTZ, which is its Preferred Optimum Temperature Zone.

URINARY SYSTEM
The kidney of the snake is a more primitive structure than that of the mammal and lies in the posterior third of the body.

Waste products follow a different metabolic pathway than that in humans; the 'urine' that snakes produce is usually solid, and white or pale yellow in colour. It is passed at the same time as the dark-coloured solid faeces.

Snakes have no urinary bladder, but can use the last part of the gastrointestinal tract for the same purpose.

OWNING A SNAKE
Snakes can make excellent and absorbing pets. They do not bark and keep the neighbours awake. They do not need to be taken for walks every day, and smaller species such as Garter Snakes and Milk Snakes cost little to feed.

Common Boa: The more you handle a snake, the tamer it will become.

Once the initial vivarium and equipment has been paid for, they do not cost much to maintain.

On the other hand, you cannot cuddle a snake – you can hardly expect a snake to come to meet you when you return home from work. However, there is no doubt that snakes have their own peculiar charm.

The more that you handle a snake, the tamer it will become. Experienced owners know that snakes come to recognise different people and behave differently with those that they know.

All snakes are carnivores. You will have to get used to handling food items such as dead mice, rats or fish. You will have to develop a routine to clean and maintain the vivarium and keep up that routine for years.

Most commonly kept species can be easily bred in captivity.

HEALTH INSURANCE

In the same way that it is possible to buy health insurance policies for dogs and cats, some insurance companies are now able to offer cover for a pet snake too.

These policies will cover veterinary fees arising from accident or disease and a variety of other possible expenses such as third-party protection if your pet causes damage to other people or to property. If the fear of a large veterinary bill concerns you, then it might be wise to buy one of these policies to give you peace of mind.

HUMAN HEALTH CONCERNS

Every snake owner should be aware of one or two concerns regarding their own health.

SALMONELLA

It must be assumed that every reptile is carrying Salmonella bacteria, even if there are no signs that it is ill.

Salmonella come in a variety of types and many are capable of causing disease in other animals, including man. The organism is shed intermittently, so a negative test does not guarantee that a reptile is free of Salmonella and there is no treatment that can guarantee to cure one that tests positive.

The problem is managed instead by exercising common sense and obeying basic hygiene rules

- Always wash your hands after you have been handling a snake, or any of the contents of the vivarium.

- Allocate water bowls and cleaning materials for snake use only and do not mix them with items used for yourself or your family.
- Certain groups, such as young children, expectant mothers, those on medication that suppresses their immune system, and those that are HIV positive, are at particular risk.
- Never kiss your pet snake or put your fingers near your mouth or eyes while handling it.

Boa Constrictor: It is important to observe rules of hygiene when handling a snake.

The Reticulated Python has a propensity to bite.

- Never allow your snake to roam over areas, such as kitchen worktops, where food is prepared or eaten.

  Although Salmonellosis can be a serious condition in humans, the risk must be kept in proportion.
  Disease contracted from pet reptiles is rare. You are far more likely to become infected from eating undercooked meat or eggs.
  The observance of simple hygiene rules should ensure that you do not add to the statistics of this emotive disease.

BITES
Like pet dogs, most snakes will bite, given the right provocation. Young hatchlings will often strike at anything that moves. These youngsters are at the early stages of learning life's rules and, if it moves, it just might be edible.
  Such bites are usually not painful. The teeth are tiny and, even if they do penetrate the skin, there will be nothing more than pin pricks. The snake will soon learn that you are too big to eat.
  It is important to wash the wound well with disinfectant soap

Burmese Python: Think carefully before committing yourself to snake ownership.

to prevent it becoming infected.

Older snakes may bite if you wiggle hands and fingers near their head in circumstances where they are expecting to be fed, especially if you have just been handling their food and they pick up the smell.

Bites from larger snakes can be more problematical. They are more likely to bite and hold on, rather than giving a quick nip and letting go. A large snake is more likely to protect its head by throwing coils of its body over its head, making it hard to get the bite released.

Some species of snakes are known to be more aggressive in this regard. Reticulated Pythons, for example, have a reputation for being big snakes with a propensity to bite.

Burmese Pythons are equally large, but are much less likely to have an aggressive attitude to people.

Once again, common sense should be exercised to avoid provoking your pet, particularly if you have a large specimen. Always have two people in the room if you are handling a snake over five feet (1.5m) long, and use gloves or a snake hook if needed. Never let a snake coil round your neck, no matter how small and tame it may appear to be.

LIFE EXPECTANCY

Before obtaining a snake as a pet, give some serious thought to the future. Assume that once you have acquired a snake, you will be keeping it until the end of its life.

- You will have to take it with you if you move house.
- You will have to make arrangements for someone else to look after it while you are away on holiday, or if you are ill in hospital.
- You will be responsible for all the costs of feeding and maintaining your snake, plus veterinary bills if your snake becomes unwell.

Snakes are not everyone's favourite pet and you will want to be sure that you have the agreement of the owner of your home and the people that you live with before the new resident moves in.

How long do snakes live? Well, that depends on the species. Generally, you can expect a pet snake to live in the region of 10 to 30 years.

FINDING OUT MORE

There are herpetology groups in most parts of the world. Some of them are branches of larger groups such as the International Herpetological Society (IHS) and some are independent.

Members will vary from experienced snake keepers with a large collection of several different species that breed regularly, to schoolchildren with their first reptile pet.

Most clubs will hold regular meetings on all sorts of snake topics and they can be a useful source of information and advice for the beginner.

Snake Species

There are more than 1700 different species of snake and some of them are more suitable to keep as pets than others. Listed below are some of the species that make the best pets.

In a general book of this nature it is not possible to give a detailed description of the husbandry of all the different snakes that are kept as pets. You should consult more specialised books on your particular species.

No description can do justice to the real thing, so you should try to take a look at the sort of snakes available before making your choice. Visit zoos, pet shops and reptile shows and talk to as many experienced keepers as you can.

Snakes come from a variety of habitats. Some live in the ocean where they may only surface once in two hours to draw breath. Others live in trees, up mountains, in jungles or deserts, in houses and farmland. They are found from the Arctic and Antarctic Circles to the Equator.

Some snakes grow no bigger than 60 cms (24 ins) while others may grow as big as a three-storey house.

There are plenty of snakes to choose from, but it is essential to know what you are taking on before making a descision.

THE BEST CHOICES

ROYAL PYTHON

This snake originally came from West Africa and, while some are still imported, many are now captive-bred.

Royal Pythons are usually docile and can be rather shy. The vivarium needs to be quiet with plenty of hiding places. Their defensive reaction is to curl into a ball, hiding their head inside the coils – hence their other name of Ball Python.

The body is thick-set and few

Royal Python: A shy snake that needs plenty of hiding places.

specimens grow much longer than 1.5 m (5 ft). The skin colour is an attractive pattern of brown, tan and black blotches.

Although Royal Pythons can climb, most seem to prefer to live at ground level and so do not need a tall vivarium. Being a relatively inactive snake, vivaria do not need to be particularly spacious.

Some specimens are reluctant feeders and ingenuity may be needed to persuade them to eat, especially when they are young. Their natural diet is rodents.

Royal Pythons can be kept in groups, and are relatively easy to breed in captivity.

GARTER SNAKE

Garter Snakes come from North America with a range that extends as far north as Canada. This is a small, slender snake (60 cm/24 inches long) that can move surprisingly quickly.

The Garter Snake is black, with prominent yellow stripes running down the body. In some specimens these yellow stripes are edged with red.

Most are docile and easy to feed. In the wild, they live near water and feed primarily on fish. Feeding them fish in captivity can give rise to thiamine deficiency (see Chapter Seven). They can

GARTER SNAKES

The Garter Snake is a small, slender snake that lives near water in the wild.

New Mexico Garter Snake.

Red Sided Garter Snake.

usually be persuaded to eat rodents instead. Rubbing a piece of fish over the outside of the mouse may help persuade a reluctant Garter Snake to eat.

A vivarium temperature of 20 to 25 degrees C (65 to 75 degrees F) should be sufficient. Living so far north, Garter Snakes are well used to a hard winter and will hibernate through it.

You need to simulate a change in seasons (see Chapter Six) in the vivarium if you want Garter Snakes to breed in captivity.

MILK SNAKE

There are 25 different subspecies of Milk Snake, with a startling variety of different colours and patterns. Most have rings of black, yellow and red that are repeated in a regular fashion along the body.

They live in similar areas to the poisonous Coral Snake and it is thought that they developed this colour pattern in order to mimic their venomous cousin. If animals learned to recognise a Coral Snake and thus avoid it they probably left Milk Snakes alone too.

Sinaloan Milk Snake: This snake prefers to burrow rather than climb.

Their average life span is 10 to 15 years. In the wild they live in open woods and fields. They prefer to burrow rather than climb, so the vivarium need not be particularly tall.

Milk Snakes grow to about 1m (3 feet) and are often rather shy. Provide plenty of hiding places in the vivarium and use a floor material that permits burrowing. They will become tamer with regular handling.

In their wild home of southern North America they will eat other snakes and lizards, but they will feed readily on mice in captivity. Being natural snake eaters, it is not unknown for one Milk Snake to eat another. If you want to keep more than one in a vivarium, take them to a separate enclosure to be fed singly. The vivarium needs to have a temperature range of 25 to 30 degrees C (75 to 85 degrees F). An adult Milk Snake needs a vivarium at least 1m (3 feet) long and 60 cm (2 feet) wide.

KING SNAKE

King Snakes come from the same parts of America as the Milk Snake and belong to the same family. Subfamily members tend to be called after their region of origin, for example, the California King Snake and the Florida King Snake.

They grow up to 2 m (6 feet) long and make excellent pets. They come in a range of colours, from

KING SNAKES

In the wild, King Snakes prey on other snakes.

Mountain King Snake.

Albino California King Snake.

black with speckles of yellows and golds, to black with yellow or white rings. Albinos also occur. Records exist of King Snakes living as long as 23 years in captivity.

Vivaria should be a similar size as those needed for a Milk Snake and provided with a similar temperature gradient. The temperature in the vivarium should drop to 70 degrees F at night. Being a shy snake, the King needs two shelters – one at the cool end of the cage and one near the warm end. Provide a water bowl big enough for the snake to soak in.

In the wild, King Snakes will readily eat other snakes and are said to be immune to the venom of some poisonous ones. In captivity they will usually thrive on dead rats and mice.

Burmese Python: A big snake that needs spacious accommodation.

BURMESE PYTHON

Adult Burmese Pythons are big snakes. They can easily grow to 6 m (19 feet) and be so heavy that it takes two people to lift them.

Do not be fooled by the 50 cm (18 ins) hatchling in the pet shop. In a few years, this will grow to be a whopper and you will have taken on the responsibility of looking after it for up to 20 years. Reptile rescue centres are full of unwanted large pythons.

Having said all that, Burmese Pythons can be very exciting snakes to keep. The normal colour is brown, with a network of paler bands. In captivity, colour mutations have appeared and albinos, which are cream with a yellow band pattern, are often available.

Being a big snake, they require a big vivarium. Converting part of a room or a cupboard is best. Their preferred temperature range is 25 to 30 degrees C (75 to 85 degrees F) with a drop at night. Coming from tropical forests, they prefer a high humidity and like to climb.

Burmese Pythons will also swim, so a large water container should be included in the set-up. They often defecate in the water,

23

which means that this must be cleaned regularly. While young Burmese Pythons will eat rats or mice, older ones will need to be fed on dead rabbits, piglets or young lambs.

Providing a menu to match the fast growth rate and large size of this snake can be quite expensive and this factor also needs to be considered before you buy one.

BOA CONSTRICTOR

Boa Constrictors are distinctive snakes with a broad head. They can grow up to at least 3 m (10 feet) long. The front end is a dark cream colour with large brown blotches that sometimes become redder near the tail end.

The Boa's home ranges include Central and South America where they inhabit dry wood and

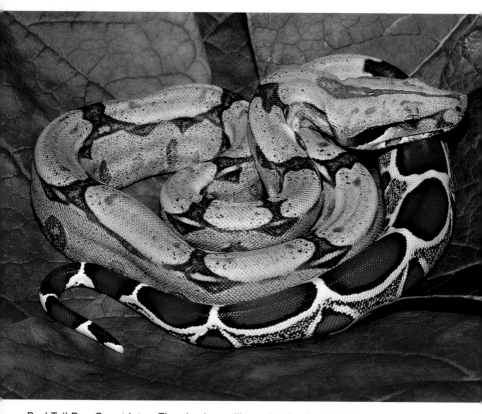

Red Tail Boa Constrictor: The vivarium will need to be fitted with branches for climbing.

Carolina Corn Snake: An excellent choice for the novice snake keeper.

scrubland. They are good climbers and the vivarium should be fitted with stout branches to support what will become quite a heavy snake.

Once again, these snakes are rodent feeders and readily eat dead mice and rats.

CORN SNAKE

Corn Snakes have been bred in captivity for years and now come in a bewildering variety of colours, usually including lots of reds and oranges.

They originate from the southern USA where their habit of hunting small rodents in cornfields gave them their name. Adult Corn Snakes are 1 to 2m (3 to 6 feet) long, with a slender build. In captivity, they will live up to 20 years, readily eating dead mice and rats.

Most Corn Snakes are placid reptiles that are easy to look after. They make an excellent choice for a first time snake keeper.

These are burrowers rather than climbers, so the vivarium does not need to be particularly tall, but it does need to be secure. Corn Snakes are veritable Houdinis.

A vivarium temperature of around 25 to 30 degrees C (75 to 85 degrees F) is ideal.

SNAKES TO AVOID

VENOMOUS SPECIES

Under the Dangerous Wild Animals Act it is illegal to keep venomous snakes without having a special licence. These are not easy to obtain.

You have to have special containment facilities, which satisfy exacting requirements. You must have access to antivenom to treat anyone who is accidentally bitten. These medicines can be very expensive, quickly go out of date and have to be replaced.

An estimated 25,000 people a year die from venomous snakebites. There are plenty of fascinating non-venomous species to choose from without all this trouble.

BAD-TEMPERED SPECIES

Some species such as the Reticulated Python and the Anaconda are renowned for their aggressive nature. They are both big snakes and an attack from either of them has got to be serious.

Unfortunately, the rescue facilities for unwanted reptiles are full of such specimens that have become too much for the original owner to handle.

GIANT SNAKES

Snakes that will become huge when they are fully grown start off as pretty small hatchlings. What may eventually grow to a length of 6m (20 feet), and weigh more than a man, starts life small enough to fit in your hand.

You should only consider owning one of these snakes if you have had lots of experience with smaller species, have lots of money to spend on a big vivarium and can give a guaranteed commitment for years to come.

CITES-LISTED SPECIES

The Convention on the International Trade in Endangered Species (CITES) includes lists of snakes that are rare or endangered.

There are different categories depending on the severity of the problem and different rules apply to each sort.

Obtaining these species can be expensive and difficult, and you may have to satisfy detailed rules about keeping, breeding and moving them.

If all you want is an interesting pet, it would be better to look at some of the more common species of snake that are readily available and captive-bred.

3 *Buying A Snake*

When you have decided on the species of snake you would like to own, the next step is to locate a reputable source and find a healthy specimen.

Do not buy trouble. If there is a weak and weedy-looking specimen on offer, it is better to pass it by and look for something better.

Snakes produce large numbers of eggs and, if all of them survived to adulthood and bred, then the world would be knee-deep in snakes. Nature compensates by accepting that most of the eggs from any particular batch will be lost, by dying before they are hatched, by being eaten or by

Baird's Rat Snake: Get off to a good start by buying a healthy specimen.

failing to adapt, grow and reproduce.

You want to buy a snake from the top of the class that has the best chance of a long, healthy and productive life in your care.

SNAKES FOR SALE

Snakes that are offered for sale will have come from one of three general backgrounds.

WILD-CAUGHT

Snakes are captured from their wild habitat, kept in a holding facility, shipped round the world and offered for sale.

Throughout the world, numbers of snake species in the wild are declining. All the popular species that are kept as pets can now be bred in captivity and it really is no longer acceptable to buy wild-caught specimens as pets.

Many such snakes on offer will have had a traumatic journey to the point of sale, perhaps being maintained in crowded, unhygienic conditions without proper food and water for long periods.

It is inevitable that a number of wild-caught specimens will harbour parasites and diseases that multiply in captivity to life-threatening levels.

CAPTIVE-FARMED

Expectant female snakes are caught in the wild at around the time of egg laying. They are kept captive until the eggs are laid and then, perhaps, released back into the wild.

CAPTIVE-BRED

The parents have mated in captivity, the eggs have been incubated artificially and the young raised to sale age.

Captive-bred specimens are far more likely to be easy to feed, adapted to captivity, free of parasites and free of disease.

Ask to handle the snake on offer and have a good look at it.

SIGNS OF GOOD HEALTH

Check out the following signs which will give a good indication of a snake's health and wellbeing.

- Both eyes should look the same – bright, clear and free of any discharges.
- The snake should have a strong grip on your hand or fingers.
- The snake should breathe without opening its mouth.
- There should be no visible blemishes or scars.
- Look closely under the chin for any sign of mites.

- When you put the snake back in the cage, check your hands to see if any mites have been left behind.

QUESTIONS TO ASK

Before committing yourself to buying a snake, you should find out the following points:

- Has the snake been eating regularly and has it been fed recently? Can you see feeding records?
- Where has the snake come from and how long has the vendor had it? Try to avoid wild-caught snakes.
- What is the sex of the snake? You may want to breed from it later so this fact needs to be established (see Sexing, page 31).
- Ask for a weight and shedding record. Young snakes should put on weight steadily and shed regularly.

PRIVATE SALE

Snakes can be bought from a variety of sources. You may know someone who has successfully incubated eggs and has some hatchlings to sell. They will be able to give a good history of the young ones' health records and

Staff at a specialist reptile shop should be able to give you advice on caring for your snake.

you will probably be able to look at the parents to see what your new purchase will become.

There are many herpetology clubs that hold regular meetings. This can be a good place to learn about snake keeping as well as to meet locals who may have stock for sale.

Many snakes used to be sold from reptile shows held in various locations. Gathering lots of snakes from different areas into one location may not be a good idea from a health point of view and there has been a view expressed by some authorities that such shows should not be allowed.

The hatchling must be able to eat on his own.

However, shows are a good opportunity to see what the different species of snakes look like, even if you do not buy there.

REPTILE SHOPS

In some areas there are speciality reptile pet shops. The best of these keep and breed their own snakes in order to stock the shop.

They are likely to have staff with a genuine interest in herpetology who will be able to give you lots of advice on keeping your new pet fit and well. They will also stock a wide range of vivarium equipment and accessories.

Some of the larger pet superstores have now stopped selling reptiles. With a large staff whose members change frequently, it is difficult to ensure that there are always good, experienced people to look after the stock and offer authoritative advice to prospective purchasers.

MAIL ORDER

Some speciality shops sell by mail order and will be willing to send stock to you by special carrier. You will need to know exactly what you want before you order it and there will, of course, be no opportunity to discuss the purchase with the seller directly.

You will have to have faith in the supplier to send you a healthy animal. These suppliers advertise in the various magazines devoted to reptile keeping and increasingly have a presence on the Internet.

REPTILE RESCUES

If you are interested in taking on an older snake, there are rescue centres which take in unwanted or abandoned reptiles. They will be delighted to supply you with one once they are convinced that you have suitable facilities and knowledge to look after it.

AGE TO BUY

Most snakes are sold as hatchlings. Few mother snakes take much care of their offspring once they hatch, so newborn snakes are usually well able to set off on life's road on their own.

However, before you take charge of your new purchase, you should make sure that two things have happened:

* That the newborn snake has shed its skin for the first time. This usually takes place within a few days of hatching. Many specimens will not feed until this has happened.
* That it has started to feed on its own and without assistance.

It is better if newly-hatched snakes have already learned to feed before you get them. It is one less thing to worry about with your new charge.

SEXING

In most snake species there is little external difference between males and females.

If you are only planning to keep a single snake, it may not matter which one you have and many snake keepers, in fact, never know whether they have bought a male or a female.

The usual technique for finding out the sex of a snake is by probing for hemipenes. Both male and female snakes have a small pocket either side of the cloaca running under the skin towards the tail. In the male this is much

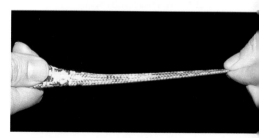

A female tail.

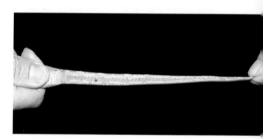

A male tail.

deeper. It is possible to pass a probe into the pocket to measure its depth.

The probe must be sterilised to prevent infection. It must be lubricated, but it is advisable to use water. Most medical lubricants are spermicidal and you do not want to render your prize breeding male infertile.

Great care must be taken to be gentle. The use of a sexing probe is not something to undertake on your own if you have not first been properly instructed in how to use it.

THE HOME-COMING

Well-prepared owners will have a vivarium set up ready for the new snake when he arrives home (see Chapter Four: Setting Up Home).

Place the new arrival in his new home and leave him well alone for several days to give the snake a chance to settle.

At first he will be shy and nervous. He will want to have a good look round the vivarium and may be scared of things happening outside his vivarium in the same room. He may only emerge from hiding at night.

After a few days' peace and quiet, you can try feeding him. If he does not take a meal when it is first offered, do not be too despondent. Try again in a few days with fresh food.

Once the new arrival has started eating on his own, you can try taking him out to get used to being handled. Remember not to try handling snakes that have fed recently. The stress may make them regurgitate the food.

Young snakes have to learn what is food and what is not. They may strike at anything moving near them, including your hand or finger. These are not usually serious bites. The snake strikes and lets go before you have even realised what is happening.

If blood has been drawn, it is best to wash the wound well with antiseptic. Most specimens will soon learn that biting humans does not lead to a full stomach and they give up the activity.

4 *Setting Up Home*

Vivaria for snakes come in a huge range of styles. Temporary accommodation for a hatchling may be as small as a plastic food container. A permanent home for a Burmese Python may be a whole room converted into a snake palace.

If you are a handyman, you may build a suitable snake home yourself, or you can buy the ready-made article from a specialist supplier.

The general principle is to provide an environment that mimics as closely as possible that which the particular species would find in the wild. This has to be tempered by what is practical and affordable.

TYPES OF ACCOMMODATION

Keep in mind that all animal cages need to be cleaned. You are more likely to do this frequently and well if you can do it easily and quickly. There should be good, wide access to the inside of the vivarium, with all the contents being removable.

Glass or plastic fish tanks make useful instant vivaria. They are cheap and easy to clean, but do have a couple of disadvantages.

- Firstly, ventilation may be poor. Try turning them on their side and fitting a ventilated door at the front.
- Secondly, living in a transparent tank does not give much privacy and shy species will be stressed. The solution is to mask at least two of the sides on the outside to limit visibility. If you use pictures of desert or jungle to do this, they will help show off your pet to best advantage.

Vivaria can be made up from plastic or fibreglass water tanks. Holes can be made for electrical equipment and to permit ventilation. Once again, placing

HOUSING YOUR SNAKE

Buy the biggest vivarium you can afford, obviously bearing in mind the size your snake will become.

A large vivarium suitable for the bigger snakes, such as a Boa.

▲ *If you are new to snake-keeping, you will probably start with a small vivarium.*

◀ *A medium-sized vivarium can make an attractive feature in a living room.*

the tank on its side will at least allow your pet to have a view. Sliding ventilated or glass doors can be fitted over the opening.

Vivaria can be constructed from wood. Bear in mind that you will be using water and disinfectant to clean it, so bare surfaces should be sealed with paint or varnish that is guaranteed non-toxic.

Allow any such finishes to dry thoroughly before placing your snake in the container. You do not want your pet to be breathing in the fumes.

Ventilation grills should be fitted at floor level, and at the top of the tank.

Melamine-coated boards make a hygienic construction material. All corners and joints can be sealed with non-toxic bathroom or fish tank sealant.

Some snake keepers house burrowing species in a cage with a hole in the floor and access to a shallow subfloor compartment in which they can hide. The subfloor is constructed as a drawer unit that can be pulled open from the outside if the occupant refuses to come back up the hole when you want him to.

VENTILATION

Fresh air is vital for health, and many vivaria have poor air circulation. Most toxic gases are heavy and will sink to the floor of the tank where your pet lives. Respiratory disease is a common reason for trips to the vet.

Large, escape-proof ventilation grills should be fitted both at floor level as well as at the top of the tank to allow good circulation of fresh air. You may even consider the use of a fan.

Do not let the need to conserve heat in the vivarium restrict the exchange of fresh air. It is better to spend a few extra pence on the heating bill than a few extra pounds at the vet's surgery to treat respiratory disease.

HEATING

Heating can be provided in many ways.

- If you have a lot of snakes, you may warm up the whole room

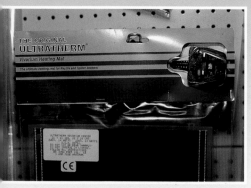

Heat mats should be placed at the side of the tank, using insulation to direct heat into the vivarium. ▲

A thermostat will control the internal temperature. ▶

to the reptiles' preferred environmental temperature.
- Incandescent heat bulbs can be fitted in the vivarium ceiling.
- Infra-red ceramic bulbs can be used in this way too.
- Heat mats should be placed on the side of the vivarium, not on the bottom. Then, if things go wrong and the device overheats, the snake has the opportunity to move away. Place insulation behind the mat to direct heat into the vivarium.
- Proprietary heaters are available which are moulded into the shape of rocks or boulders.
- Big cages can be warmed with tubular ceramic heaters.

All heating systems must be protected with cut-outs that switch the power off if they get too hot. The more powerful ones must also be controlled by a thermostat placed in the vivarium at the level that the snake will be living so that the heater will be switched on and off as required.

Many snakes will experience a natural drop in temperature during the night in the wild and you should try and duplicate this in the vivarium. Timers will allow the heater to be programmed so that it gradually drops to a cooler temperature during the night and warms up slowly again in the morning.

If some of the heating power in the vivarium comes from lamps which give off light too, it is important to make sure that these dim at night to give the snake a period of darkness. Twenty-four-hour light is stressful.

Snakes seem to have an amazing facility for lying in contact with hot surfaces and getting burned. A wire cage should protect any heat source that becomes warm enough to do damage, so that the snake is kept at a safe distance. Even lights in the ceiling that you think are out of reach should be covered in this way. Some snakes are agile climbers.

Different snakes maintain their temperature in different ways. Tree dwellers, such as Chondropythons, like to bask under a hot bulb on the ceiling simulating a warm sun.

Burrowers, such as Corn Snakes, prefer to lie in a tunnel under a surface warmed by a heat mat, as they would do under a sunny spot of soil. The heating system that you install in your vivarium should duplicate the inhabitant's natural habitat.

HEAT GRADIENTS

Snakes are just like people, in that sometimes they feel too hot and sometimes too cold. They adjust

The vivarium should have an area where the snake can go to cool down.

Snakes will become stressed if lighting is left on 24 hours a day.

to this situation by moving towards or away from the heating source. Snakes are said to have a preferred temperature range and this range will be different for different species. Ideally, the vivarium should have a hot spot that is maintained at the top of the preferred temperature range and a cool spot at the bottom of the range. This gives the occupant the chance to move in order to stay comfortable.

LIGHTING

The lighting required in your vivarium will vary with the species you are keeping.

Corn Snakes that live underground for much of the time will be happy with some pretty dim lighting. Rosy Boas that come from a semi-desert environment will need much brighter, full-spectrum lights.

A timer should control all lights so that they dim in the evening and brighten again in the morning. Manipulation of the photoperiod is one of the main ways to bring many species into breeding condition (see Chapter Six: Breeding Snakes).

Some reptiles require lighting that emits energy in the ultraviolet range in order to make vitamin

D. Most snakes will obtain all the vitamin D that they need from the food they eat. But if you are keeping a snake that comes from a desert environment, it might be worth using a full-spectrum, or ultraviolet, light to mimic the desert sun as closely as possible.

Normal electric lighting flickers on and off fifty times a second – too fast for us to see. But some reptiles seem to be able to perceive this flicker, and may find life under what looks, to them, like a disco strobe light, rather stressful.

SECURITY
Most people who have kept reptiles for any length of time will tell you their escape stories. Snakes seem able to squeeze through the smallest of spaces and a few hours patrolling the confines of a vivarium will often reveal a hole for your pet to get through.

All access doors should have a catch or bolt. If there are children in the house it might even be worth getting a lock and key fitted. Although there are stories of snakes turning up again fit, fat and well after months living free, there are lots of other stories that you do not hear, where the escapee was never found.

DECOR
This will vary with the species and your wishes about how the vivarium looks.

Pieces of plastic pipe and old food containers of appropriate size

The vivarium should be fitted with a secure lock.

Interior decor should provide shelter, and be easy to clean.

make practical hides that are easy to clean and disinfect, but may not look very smart.

Disposable alternatives include the tubes from the inside of toilet paper or kitchen roll.

Pet shops sell shelters made of bark that look attractive but may provide excellent hiding places for snake mites and can be very difficult to sterilise completely.

You may be able to make up your own shelters from modelling clay, plastic or wood.

Large, colourful rocks look good in a desert set-up and can be easily scrubbed clean and sterilised.

When you place them in the vivarium make sure they are stable. Snakes have been injured by stones that have become dislodged and fallen on them. Rocks with a rough surface will be used as an abrasive to help shed skin.

INTRODUCING PLANTS
Jungle-dwelling species look wonderful against a background of real plants, but such a vivarium is very difficult to maintain. The warm and humid environment may not suit many houseplants. Others will grow prolifically and take over the whole vivarium. Snakes climbing in the branches may damage the foliage and, if you do have a health problem with your animals, it will be

Real plants look attractive in the vivarium, but they are difficult to maintain.

Logs or branches should be securely fitted for the climbing species.

impossible to sterilise the vegetation.

If you do decide to use real plants, make sure they are non-poisonous. A surprising number of houseplants have toxic effects. Keep the plants in a flowerpot covered by the substrate on the floor of the vivarium. That way they can be removed if necessary without being uprooted.

Bear in mind that the vivarium is primarily a home for your snake. It will be hard to see the reptile in a tank full of rampant plant growth.

Some reptile keepers who use real plants in their vivaria keep a stock of plants that are rotated: a few weeks in the vivarium and then a spell outside, perhaps in a greenhouse where they are easier to tend.

Artificial plants form an alternative to real ones. The best ones are very realistic. They are easy to clean and disinfect and can be moved around to vary the layout.

CLIMBING FEATURES

Climbing species can be accommodated in a variety of ways. Natural logs or branches can be laid into the higher reaches of the cage or you may choose to use metal or plastic constructions. Make sure the structure is secure and cannot be accidentally knocked down.

WATER ELEMENTS

Snakes that come from a humid environment, or near lakes and rivers, will benefit from a water feature. At its most simple, this will be a bowl of water in the floor of the cage. It can be sunk into the substrate so that its lip is level with the floor. Many snakes will bathe in these pools.

Remember that reptiles can hold their breath for many minutes and a snake that has been lying at the bottom of the water bowl for ages may not necessarily be dead.

Some species use water bowls as toilets. These will need to be cleaned frequently. It is also now possible to buy waterfall features with pumps that circulate water from a pool at the bottom. These devices help to keep the water clean and raise the humidity. There are even miniature foggers to make your mini-jungle really steamy.

SUBSTRATES

The ideal floor material for a snake cage does not exist. Everything that has been tried seems to have advantages and disadvantages.

The final material selected will depend a little on which snake you keep. If your pet is one that likes to burrow underground, such as a

Corn Snake, being kept in a vivarium with a solid floor where it cannot hide itself will be stressful.

On the other hand, if you have a snake that normally lives in trees, such as a Green Tree Python, you do not need to worry so much about what is on the floor.

In the wild, snakes will have a territory much bigger than any vivarium. When they empty their bowel, it may be months before they come that way again. Potentially harmful bacteria and parasites in the faeces may have died long before their host comes back.

The situation in a vivarium is very different. Ground-dwelling snakes live in intimate contact with anything on the floor of the cage and hygiene needs to be maintained to a high standard if health problems are to be avoided. As soon as the floor of the vivarium gets dirty or soiled it must be cleaned out.

NEWSPAPER

Newspaper is readily available, cheap and works well as a cage liner. It is easy to see when it gets dirty and is quick and easy to change.

Snake keepers, who previously

CHOOSING A SUBSTRATE

Newspaper: Readily available, and easy to change.

Woodchip: Looks attractive, but can be ingested by accident.

Moss: A natural solution, but maintenance can be difficult.

Sand: Ideal for desert-dwelling species, but can be ingested with food.

kept their pets on bark chips, will be amazed how quickly the floor of the cage looks grubby when they change to newspaper.

Modern newspaper production methods, using heat and chemicals, mean that fresh newspaper is almost sterile – a hygienic solution that is especially suitable if your pet is recovering from an injury or disease.

There may be some concern about the inks rubbing off the paper and onto your snake, but I am not aware of this ever having caused a problem.

Occasionally, it may be possible to obtain blank newsprint before it has been printed and this would obviously be better still.

A clean, white sheet on the floor of the cage probably looks better than a mix of adverts, models and footballers. Using several layers may provide burrowing snakes with somewhere to hide between the sheets.

ARTIFICIAL TURF

Plastic grass was originally developed for use on all-weather sport pitches, but has now found a use as a low-maintenance covering for the garden patio or even as a door mat. Many garden centres sell it by the metre.

You need three pieces, cut to fit the floor of the vivarium. One piece is in use, one is soaking in a bucket of disinfectant and one is a spare.

The initial investment will last you for ages and a fresh green lawn on the floor of the cage will set off colourful snakes beautifully. If it is changed as soon as it gets dirty, it fulfils the hygiene requirements, although it may not be much use as a burrowing material.

BARK CHIPS

Bark chips from various types of tree, and in various sizes, have been a popular choice of material to spread on the floor of the cage.

It looks natural, permits burrowing and, if only part of the vivarium is dirty, you do not need to remove the whole lot at once.

There are, however, disadvantages to using this material. Being a similar colour to snake faeces, it may be difficult to see when it gets dirty. It provides a wonderful environment for snake mites or worm eggs to live in and it is not recyclable.

Occasionally, a piece of bark will get stuck to a prey item and be eaten along with the food. Snake digestive juices are not able to break down bark and most reptile vets will have performed post-mortem examinations on snakes that have died because their intestine is blocked by bark.

Some bark has been sterilised before it reaches the shop. If it has not, there may be microscopic – and not so microscopic – animals living within the material. These also may pose a risk to your pet.

GRAVEL, PEBBLES AND SAND

These cheap materials can also look good in a vivarium set up for desert-dwelling species. Make sure that sand cannot get stuck to food items, or it will be eaten in the same way as bark chips and can cause similar problems.

Larger-grained material such as gravel can be washed in a sieve, boiled in water or baked in an oven and recycled as sterile material. For animals that inhabit a warm and humid environment, it may be difficult to keep the vivarium moist enough with these as substrates.

CORN KERNELS

Dried corn kernels seem to be just as indigestible as gravel if they

accidentally get into a snake's digestive tract.

CLEANING

In the wild, most snakes have a home range that is much larger than even the biggest captive environment.

As I said earlier, if they pass urine or faeces in one particular place, it may be ages before they pass that way again. Rain and wind will have dispersed it before they do.

In the same way, they are most unlikely to be breathing in air that has recently left the lungs of another snake.

This is not the case in captivity. Hence the need for high standards of hygiene.

A high standard of hygiene must be observed in the vivarium.

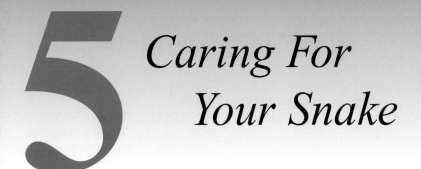

5 Caring For Your Snake

All snakes are carnivores, feeding on fish, birds or small mammals, depending on the species. A few specialists even eat eggs.

Snakes cannot chew pieces off their prey. They have to swallow them whole. As a general guide, food items should be no larger in diameter than the thickest part of the snake's body.

THE SNAKE DIET

Food items are sold in various sizes:

- Lance fish: small whole fish for fish-eating snakes
- Pinkies: newborn mice
- Fuzzies: double the size with hair just starting to grow
- Half-grown mice
- Full-grown mice
- Rat pups
- Half-grown rats
- Full-grown rats
- Rabbits
- Chicks
- Quail.

In the wild, food items will be caught and eaten alive, but this is completely unacceptable for pet snakes and may, in fact, be illegal. Terrified live prey species may turn on a snake and inflict quite serious bite injuries.

Commercial breeders raise mice, rats and rabbits as snake food. They are humanely killed, frozen whole and sold either through pet shops or by mail order. Domestic freezers will keep such food fresh for the same time as meat for human consumption.

When you are ready to feed the snake, take one or two items out of the freezer and bring them up to room temperature. Snakes possess heat sensors that can tell the temperature of their prey to within a fraction of a degree.

In the wild, this may help them to avoid eating sick animals that may have a fever. In captivity, it means that food is more attractive if you warm it up to about body temperature, perhaps by soaking in a bowl of warm water or by brief use of a microwave oven.

Offer the food to the snake and remove anything that has not been eaten within twelve hours.

Movement will often induce a snake to strike. Try holding the food in a pair of tweezers or long forceps and moving it back and forth in front of the snake. Do not just use fingers. The strike, when it comes, may hit you by mistake.

If the thought of all this puts you off, you might consider the new types of snake foods now being produced in a rather more anonymous sausage format. Ask your pet shop what they have available.

Snakes that are stressed will often regurgitate a recently eaten meal so, unless your pet is very tame, it is probably best not to handle him for a couple of days after he has been fed.

Once the visible lump of the food no longer shows through the body wall, it is safe to pick him up again.

Reluctance to feed is a common problem in captive snakes (see Chapter Six).

WATER

All snakes should be provided with a bowl of water and this must be changed regularly to keep it fresh. Large bowls will double as a bath for those that like a swim and will also increase the humidity in the vivarium.

For very young snakes, the water should be in a shallow bowl sunk into the flooring material so that it is easy for them to reach.

VITAMIN AND MINERAL SUPPLEMENTS

Most pet shops have a bewildering array of vitamin and mineral supplements for reptiles.

By and large, as a snake keeper, you can walk past this part of the display. Whole prey species that were healthy and well fed before they were killed, and that have not languished too long in the freezer, will contain all the vitamins and minerals that a snake will need.

The only exceptions to this rule will be fish-eating snakes that refuse to be converted to a rodent diet. There is a danger of vitamin B1 deficiency from the thiaminase in the fish and it might be prudent to supplement the diet with this relatively cheap and easily available vitamin (see Chapter Seven).

Other vitamin deficiency

FEEDING YOUR SNAKE

A snake may strike when food is offered, so it is advisable to use tweezers to hold it.

The snake seizes its meal.

elastic membrane enables the snake to widen its mouth so that it can swallow its prey.

Do not handle your snake while the lump of food is still visible through the body wall.

diseases are recorded in reptiles but they are rare. Diseases caused by over-supplementation are more common and the best advice is to feed your pet a wholesome diet and only use supplements when your vet recommends them.

SHEDDING

All snakes shed their skin regularly. A young, fast-growing snake may shed as often as twice a month and an old one as little as twice a year.

Healthy snakes should shed their skin in one piece. Piecemeal shedding is often a sign that the snake is not healthy, or is living in an unsatisfactory environment.

The first signs that shedding is about to occur will be a loss of appetite. The skin colours may look duller or the snake may take on a slightly bluish/grey tint. The eyes will become cloudy. The old skin should start to shed from the tip of the nose and work backwards, turning inside out as it goes.

The snake may rub itself over rough surfaces and, for this reason, all snake vivaria should contain a large, rough stone.

The shed skin is almost transparent, initially soft but becoming brittle as it dries. Shed skin is dead tissue and should be removed from the vivarium.

The first signs of shedding may be loss of appetite and a dull skin colour.

Shed skin must be removed from the vivarium.

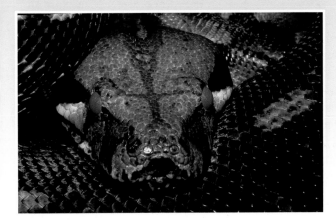

Snakes do not have eyelids, so the skin over the eyes is also shed.

Snakes do not have eyelids as we do and the skin in fact extends right across the eye as a transparent sheet.

Always check the shed skin to be sure that it includes the part over the eyes.

The shed skin mimics the scales over the snake's body and the eye-cap appears as a rather larger curved skin scale from the side of the head.

Abnormalities in the way that the skin is shed indicate a health problem (see Chapter Seven).

KEEPING THE HABITAT CLEAN

Cleanliness is an important part of looking after any animal and snakes are no different. If the vivarium smells, it needs cleaning.

- Faeces and urine (urates) should be removed as soon as you see them. Wear a glove, or use a poop-scoop. Regular cleaning needs to be undertaken as often as necessary – every week if you have several fast-growing active specimens in a small vivarium and every month if you have a single snake which is hibernating and therefore not eating.
- Some cage materials, such as newspaper on the floor, may simply be thrown away and replaced with fresh clean sheets.
- Anything that is going to go back in the vivarium and that is visibly dirty needs to be scrubbed clean first.
- Rocks and ceramic or metal water bowls can be boiled in water in an old saucepan, cooled and replaced in the vivarium.
- Plastic material that would be damaged by boiling can be soaked in a proprietary disinfectant, rinsed well, dried and returned to the vivarium. Always read and follow the instructions on the disinfectant container. If you are in any doubt, contact the manufacturer and ask if it is safe to use for cleaning pet cage furniture.
- Wooden materials such as climbing logs and hides which float in water can be scalded by pouring boiling water over them. Make sure that you do not pour boiling water over yourself at the same time.
- The vivarium itself can be cleaned with hot soapy water, then disinfected with a solution made up to the manufacturer's recommended concentration, rinsed and dried. Make sure all electrical equipment, such as heating elements and thermostats, are removed before you get them wet.
- Any materials that still smell of disinfectant after you have cleaned them should be aired first. Breathing air in a vivarium that contains disinfectant fumes will be harmful for your snake.

TEMPORARY ACCOMMODATION

What do you do with your pet while all this cleaning and disinfection is going on?

Firstly, do not worry too much about temperature. A sausage taken out of the freezer and left at room temperature takes an hour to thaw out. Anything but the tiniest of snakes will take hours to cool down from vivarium temperature to that in an average

CLEANING THE VIVARIUM

You will need to provide temporary accommodation while you are cleaning the vivarium.

Use a poop-scoop to remove soiled substrate.

The vivarium will need to be cleaned and disinfected.

living room. Your cleaning work should be finished long before this happens.

The same temperature story will apply to occasions when you take your reptile out of his home to show him to friends or to accustom him to handling.

Temporary homes for your reptile during the cleaning process include an old ice-cream tub or a bucket with a well-fitting lid, a cardboard box without any escape holes or even an old pillowcase with the top tied shut. Bags like this are also handy for taking your pet to the vet. Always make sure the snake's head is not on its way out of the neck if you are closing the bag with an elastic band. Bear in mind that snakes are great escape artists and will take any chance to go AWOL.

HANDLING

The more that you handle your snake the tamer it will become. The less you handle it the more nervous and potentially aggressive it will be. It is much easier to tame a captive-bred hatchling than an adult, and many wild-caught specimens will never become tame.

The snake should be picked up mid-body. If it is fast and active, do not hold it over a drop where it would get hurt by falling.

A snake should be picked up mid-body, and allowed to coil over your arm or hand.

Snakes are curious creatures, and most will appreciate any opportunity to explore.

If it wants to wriggle, let it run through your fingers on to your other hand. If it wants to coil, let it grip your arm or hand. Never lift a snake by the neck without supporting the rest of the body. The joint in the spine that joins the head to the neck is inherently weak in snakes and you can easily cause damage.

If the snake tries to get away from you, do not squeeze too tightly. It is easy to cause bruising or muscle injury. Few snakes like to be turned on their back and most will resist the attempt to do so.

Snakes are curious creatures and like to explore. Just watch one placed in a new vivarium. Larger specimens can be let out of the vivarium to explore a living room for a while, but under close supervision and only after a few precautions have been taken.

Remove any pets. Both dogs and cats are likely to attack a snake that they may have never seen before. Gerbils and hamsters may be seen as prey by the snake and it will be terrifying for the rodent to be threatened by a serpent through the bars of a cage that it cannot get out of.

Block all escape routes. Snakes are very good at finding the smallest hole or climbing inside furniture where you cannot reach them.

Burn injuries are common on snakes. Do not let your pet near hot radiators or fires that could harm it.

For reasons of hygiene, do not let your snake roam in the kitchen, larder or food preparation areas.

6 *Breeding Snakes*

Breeding your pets, and raising the young successfully, can be one of the most rewarding parts of snake ownership, but should not be approached lightly. There are many things to think about first.

GENERAL CONSIDERATIONS

You will need at least one male and female. Do not laugh. Female snakes of some species will lay eggs even if they have not been mated, but the eggs will be infertile and will never hatch. Even

A male and a female Boa: Determining the sex of a snake is a specialist task.

An amelanistic Corn Snake: Selective breeding can produce different shades of colour as well as specific markings.

if you keep a male and female snake together, all eggs will die if the snakes have never mated.

Determining the sex in those species where males and females look the same is usually done by probing the sacs either side of the cloaca.

This is a specialist task that needs to be done by someone who knows what they are doing and has the right tools for the job. It is easy to cause damage and hurt the snake. Most vets who treat snakes regularly will do this for you for a small fee.

You will need facilities for incubating the eggs and raising the hatchlings and you will need a market for the offspring. If your pet Python lays 107 eggs (as a Burmese Python once did), and you successfully hatch all of them, you will want to be sure that you have access to good caring homes for them all.

COLOUR MORPHS

With many species, such as the Burmese Python and the Corn Snake, there is a lot of interest in producing snakes of different colours.

Changes in the chromosomes

will produce albinos (those with no colour at all), amelanistics (light-coloured snakes) or anerythristics (those which lack any red colour). It is also possible to select for snakes showing a particular pattern, such as Corn Snakes with zigzags or Boa Constrictors with red tails.

Some people feel that this is tinkering with nature and that breeders should try and preserve the colour and appearance that the snakes had in the wild. In most cases, snakes developed their normal colouring as camouflage in their home environment and white or bright yellow ones had a poorer chance of surviving.

SPECIES AND HIGH-BREDS

Snake experts still argue over which snakes are separate species and which ones are just different races in the same species.

The simple differentiation is that animals belonging to different species will not breed together successfully. You cannot mate a cat to a dog and expect to produce any offspring. But the lines do get blurred. Horses and donkeys are separate species but, if you breed them together, you will certainly get live, healthy offspring.

In the snake world it has proved possible, for example, to mate different species of Pythons together and get live, fertile

Dot-Dash California King Snake: There is concern that breeding for colour and pattern will mean that snakes can no longer breed true to type.

young. In some cases these, in turn, have been mated with other species to produce strange mixtures of species.

In most cases, this is done to produce snakes of different colours, patterns or sizes. There is concern that, if these breeding practices become widespread, it will no longer be possible to find snakes in captivity that will breed true to the original type that was captured from the wild.

Each breeder will have to make up his own mind about which individual snakes are bred, but my personal feeling is that selective breeding should not stray too far from the original type that occurs in the wild.

There may be more important criteria to use to select your breeding stock, such as resistance to disease, a placid temperament or good adaptation to life in captivity.

CONDITIONING FOR BREEDING

In the wild, snakes will breed at the best time of year to give the young a good start in life. Young

White Lipped Python: The change of seasons is the trigger for breeding, and these conditions will need to be recreated within the vivarium.

Garter Snakes arriving in the middle of a Canadian winter are unlikely to survive, but if they appear as the frogspawn and fish fry are hatching, they will be surrounded by good things to eat.

CHANGING SEASONS

In most cases the trigger for wild snakes to breed is the changing seasons and this needs to be reproduced in the vivarium.

For tropical species, this may be related to the dry and rainy seasons but, for snakes from temperate regions, it will usually be the length of the daylight in springtime.

A female snake will feed well during the summer and autumn, hibernate through the winter and produce young the following spring. Mating may take place in the autumn as, in some species, the female will store sperm to fertilise the eggs that she makes later.

For those species that require seasonal stimuli, you need to lower the temperature and shorten the light period. Ideally, this should be done gradually and then reversed gradually after the artificial winter.

Specialist reptile shops will sell you the appropriate electronic controllers to enable this to be programmed in so that you do not have to do it all by hand.

The temperature should not drop too low or the health of the parents may suffer. Once again, the exact figures will depend on the species concerned, but a drop to about 21 degrees C (70 degrees F) should be about right.

The daylight length can be reduced to 8 hours out of 24. The artificial winter may last from 2 to 10 weeks.

During the hibernation period most snakes will stop eating, although they may remain quite active. They do not really go to sleep in the same way that hibernating mammals do.

Male and female snakes are usually kept separate, with the female being introduced into the male's vivarium when you judge that the time is right.

There may be a courtship period when the snakes twine their bodies together. In snakes such as Boas, the spurs on either side of the cloaca are used to stimulate the female.

Mating takes place by the male introducing his hemipenes into the cloaca of the female and may last several hours. Mating may be repeated several times.

Chequered Garter Snake: The male and female are kept separate until it is time to mate.

EGG-LAYERS AND LIVE-BEARERS

Not all snakes lay eggs. In some species, notably the Boas and Garter Snakes, the eggs are, in effect, incubated inside the mother and it is freshly hatched young that you first see on the outside.

Egg-laying snakes should be provided with a nest site. This may be a box big enough for the mother snake to get inside, filled with moist soil or damp sphagnum moss.

Eggs take time to form in the mother's reproductive tract and, as they enlarge, they will reduce the space left for the gastrointestinal tract. Many expectant mothers will refuse food for weeks, or even months, while they are incubating eggs. They should be handled as little as possible to avoid damaging the delicate eggs inside them.

Snakes that are born live (outside the egg) may still be encased in the egg membrane and it may be necessary to help free the young so that they can breathe. Use a pair of sharp scissors to cut the surrounding tissue without damaging the snake inside.

The eggs laid by a Corn Snake. In most cases, it is advisable to use an incubator.

EGG INCUBATION

The technique for egg incubation will depend on the species. Some Pythons, such as the Burmese, will incubate their own eggs. The mother curls round the clutch and fiercely protects them against predators.

You will also see an interesting technique that the mother uses to keep the eggs at the right temperature. Every few seconds the snake appears to have a twitch or contraction affecting the muscles along the body. This muscular work warms the snake up in the same way that it does a human in a gym. As the mother's temperature rises, so heat is conducted to the eggs that she is in contact with.

In the wild, snakes that do not incubate the eggs themselves will lay them in piles of rotting vegetation where the warmth of decay will keep them healthy.

For most pet snakes, it is better to remove the eggs from the vivarium and hatch them separately in an incubator. This can be a commercial device that you bought from a specialist manufacturer, or it can be one that you made up yourself.

INCUBATION RULES

There are a number of all-important rules to follow when incubating eggs.

TEMPERATURE

The incubation temperature is critical and needs to be maintained in a much narrower range than the vivarium for an adult snake.

A change of even a few degrees will usually kill the eggs or cause deformities in the offspring.

The exact temperature varies with the different species of snake. Generally it will be in the range of 29 to 32 degrees C (85 to 90 degrees F).

HUMIDITY

The humidity needs to be high. Between 60 and 100 per cent, depending again on the species. The developing embryo will dry out and die if the incubation medium is not wet enough.

On the other hand, if the humidity gets too high, moulds and bacteria will flourish and these can also kill eggs.

DO NOT DISTURB

The orientation of the eggs must be kept constant.

Eggs may get stuck together as they are laid, and it is important that no attempt is made to separate them.

Move the egg mass carefully to the incubator and try and keep the same side up throughout the whole process.

VENTILATION

The embryos are alive in the eggs and need a source of oxygen. The egg container needs ventilation holes and the lid should be taken off every day or two as you check the eggs to allow a change of air.

Some commercial incubators have fan-assisted ventilation.

A hatchling Corn Snake breaking out of the egg.

THE HATCHLINGS

Newborn baby Boas. The hatchlings will need to be separated and reared individually.

Baby Baird's Rat Snake: A hatchling will shed its skin after a few days – and only then will it start to feed.

THE HOME-MADE INCUBATOR

A good home-made incubator can be constructed round a large ice-cream container. Puncture holes in the lid for ventilation and to admit the electrical lead of a thermostat. Half-fill the container with vermiculite or sphagnum moss from a garden centre and add an equal weight of water.

Place the container on a heat mat with a controlling thermostat in the upper centimetre (half-inch) of the vermiculite. Surround the whole container with polystyrene or fibreglass insulation. Set this up some time before the eggs are expected, and record the temperature several times a day for a week or so, to check that the set-up is working properly.

When the eggs arrive, half-bury them in the vermiculite. Remove any that discolour or collapse. The incubation time varies from as little as 30 days to over 100 days depending on the species and the temperature. Hatching occurs over a few days although it is worth keeping eggs that have not hatched for another week or two in case there are any late arrivals.

HATCHING

Breaking out of the egg is hard work and may take some time.

Many young snakes will stay within the protection of the broken shell for another day or two before emerging into the big bad world.

Once they do become more active in the incubation chamber, they can be removed to the rearing accommodation. Hatchlings will live on the remains of the yolk sac for the first two or three weeks of life.

DYSTOCHIA

Snakes can get into trouble having babies in the same way that any other animal can. Egg-layers may become exhausted before all the eggs are laid, or there may be an extra large or deformed egg that is difficult to pass.

Eggs that remain in the mother after the date that they should have been laid will die and decay. The snake will become very ill and may well die. A check-up with the vet after egg-laying may pick up such problems before they become life-threatening.

RAISING THE OFFSPRING

Some species of snake have large litters. The babies are best kept individually so that you can be sure exactly which one produced that bowel movement in the

The hatchling needs to be feeding independently before they go to a new home.

bottom of the cage and which one ate the pinkie mouse you left there last night.

That does not mean that you have to provide each of them with a cage as elaborate as their parents – at least not to begin with. Most hatchlings will be quite happy in a simple, ventilated, plastic box with a water bowl, a hide and a heat mat under one end to give the box a temperature range near to that preferred for the species.

Some breeders use racks of shelving to hold these boxes, with labels at the front to give the husbandry details on each of the inhabitants.

Most hatchling snakes will shed their skin when they are a few days old and it is only after this has happened that they will start to feed. It can be tricky to get them started and you may need to use some of the ruses listed in Chapter Six.

Responsible breeders will want to be sure that their hatchlings are feeding well on their own before passing them on to the new owner.

Regular weighing on a gram scale will tell you if the young are thriving. There should be a steady gain in weight from the first feed onwards.

7 Health Care

Most snake keepers will need the help of a veterinary surgeon at some time. Not all vets have an interest in treating these species and, while any vet will do his best in an emergency situation, it may be worth identifying a local practitioner who is willing to see sick snakes and has some experience in their care, before you need his or her assistance. If your nearest practice does not routinely see snakes, they will usually be able to recommend another one that does.

SNAKE-FRIENDLY VETS

Preventative medicine applies just as much to snakes as it does to human beings and a trip for a check-up to a vet who has experience with reptiles may identify health concerns before they become a problem. Even if

Royal Python: It is essential to find a vet who has experience in treating snakes.

Green Tree Python: Keep a detailed record of your snake's health.

your vet gives your pet the all-clear, it may be money well spent to give you peace of mind. It will also mean that, should you later need to ring the veterinary practice for advice, they will know who you are and what animal you keep.

Pet snakes are, at most, a few generations from wild animals. They retain many of the features that protect them in the wild environment, including the ability to conceal any signs of illness or disease. In the wild, an animal that shows that it is ill also reveals itself as easy pickings for a predator. By the time that you see obvious signs of illness affecting your pet's health, the snake is probably failing fast. As a famous snake vet once said "A snake that is obviously ill is actually dying". If your snake shows clear signs of disease, get it to a vet quickly if you want to have the best chance of saving it. Snakes that are obviously ill will rarely get better on their own.

HEALTH RECORDS

If you do need to attend a vet's surgery, one of the first things that will happen is that the vet will start asking questions. When did the problem start? When did your snake last eat? Do you have a weight record for him? When did he last pass faeces? What is the temperature in the vivarium?

The snake keeper that can whip out a notebook with detailed health records for each of his snakes will delight the veterinary surgeon and improve the chances of identifying the problem and getting the correct treatment.

Vets cannot ask their patients questions; they rely heavily on what the owner can tell them in reaching a diagnosis.

QUARANTINE

Buying a new snake always involves some element of risk. Some infectious diseases are difficult to spot and others have a long incubation period. You may want to consider taking your new purchase to a vet who has an interest in treating reptiles for a check-up. Although even he will

not be able to guarantee that your new snake is healthy, he will be able to spot signs of disease that you may have missed, check for parasites and give you sound advice on how to look after your new charge.

If you already have other snakes, it is important to quarantine your new arrival. Ideally, keep it in a separate vivarium in a different room for as long as you can (at least a month) before introducing it to the rest of your collection.

Always clean and handle your new acquisition after the rest of your collection so that there is less chance of passing an infection in

If you already have snakes, it is important to quarantine a new arrival.

the new snake on to them. Keep water bowls and vivarium equipment for the new charge separate and keep an eagle eye out for signs of anything going wrong during the quarantine period.

SHEDDING

Skin may be shed in bits rather than in a single piece if the vivarium is too dry.

- Try spraying the tank with a plant sprayer filled with water once or several times a day.
- Place a large bowl of water in the tank. Some of this will evaporate in the warm atmosphere of the vivarium and the snake may even use it as a bath.

- Provide a sweatbox by filling an old ice-cream container, big enough for your snake to get inside, with wet sphagnum moss or foam chips and cutting an access hole in the side.
- Retained eye caps are best dealt with by the vet.
- Patches of old skin still stuck on the body may come loose if you place the snake, for an hour, in a pillow case that has been soaked with warm water. It gets like a Turkish bath inside and this will often hydrate the skin enough for it to slough off on its own.

  The snake will crawl round inside the bag rubbing on the material and this will also encourage the old skin to separate.

Garter Snake: Providing a bowl of water in the vivarium will aid skin-shedding.

- Snakes will often rub themselves on a large rough rock placed in the vivarium to help loosen shedding skin.

NOSE-RUBBING

Some snakes seem unable to accept that a barrier that they can see through is not one that they can slither through. They persistently rub their noses on the glass walls of the vivarium until the nose gets inflamed or even ulcerated.

One solution is to stick masking tape on the outside of the glass for a few inches up the walls. Snakes that can no longer see through the glass usually stop rubbing their nose on it.

LACK OF APPETITE

Pet snakes of species that hibernate in the wild may lose their appetite during the winter. They may or may not remain active and will usually resume eating again after a few weeks.

Other reasons for loss of appetite include:

INCORRECT ENVIRONMENT

Most snakes have a body temperature similar to that in the vivarium. If this is too low, the digestive enzymes will not work properly and, in effect, the snake develops indigestion. This is the so-called 'death zone'. The temperature is too high for the snake to hibernate and too low for it to digest its food. It will just starve to death.

INCORRECT LIGHTING

Snakes may see in ultraviolet in the same way that insects do. With the wrong lighting, food appears the wrong colour. Would you eat purple mashed potato?

Most electric lights flicker on and off 50 times a second, which is too fast for humans to see, but there is evidence that some reptiles may be able to see this flicker and may find it stressful.

Twenty-four-hour lighting is very unpleasant for people and may harm snakes too. Make sure there is a timer on the vivarium lighting to allow a night-time dark period.

TIPS TO TEMPT A RELUCTANT FEEDER

The following tips are worth trying:
- Most wild rodents are brown. Some snakes that refuse white rats and mice will eat coloured ones.
- Snakes are said to be able to detect temperature changes of

Brazilian Rainbow Boa.

0.1 degree F. Make sure that the prey item is as near live body temperature as you can manage.

- Some snakes prefer to eat in private. If its natural habit is to crawl down burrows to find food underground, it may not accept food out in the open with the whole family gazing at it.

  Try turning a flowerpot upside down, cut an entrance hole out of the rim and place the food item inside.

  Alternatively, place the food halfway down a cardboard tube, such as the inner tube which remains after a roll of kitchen towel has been used.

- Try getting the snake annoyed. Hold the prey item by the tail or in forceps and swing it backwards and forwards round the snake's head, bumping it gently on the nose.

- Find out what the snake would eat in the wild. If you have a Garter Snake which normally eats fish and you want it to eat mice, try rubbing a piece of fish over the rodent's fur so that it smells of fish instead of mouse.

- Food items that have been in the freezer a long time deteriorate. Try getting a new supply of fresh food.

- Your local pet shop may be prepared to kill humanely a live rodent so that you can offer freshly-killed prey.

- Some quite large snakes seem to prefer to eat lots of small food items rather than fewer large ones.

- At vivarium temperatures, food soon goes off and it is best to remove and discard any food that has not been eaten after a few hours.

MOUTH ROT

Mouth infections are common in snakes. They may also be associated with infections elsewhere, spreading down the airway into the lungs or up the tear duct into the eye.

Open the mouth, gently using a stiff piece of plastic such as a credit card or the shaft of a knitting needle. Normal mouths are pink and dry, or only slightly sticky.

Stomatitis ('mouth rot') appears as red or bleeding areas or raised areas of sticky yellow pus. Stomatitis is potentially fatal and you need expert veterinary help for treatment.

MITES

Snake mites make snakes itchy. Infested reptiles rub themselves on the furniture in the vivarium and may spend time soaking in the water bowl trying to drown the parasites.

Careful scrutiny with good lighting or a hand lens will show tiny white (empty) or dark (full)

Baby Columbian Rainbow Boa.

Northern Pine Snake.

spider-like creatures attached around or under skin scales. They may even run over your hand as you are handing the snake.

Snake mites can carry serious snake infections as well as making your pet's life a misery with the irritation of their bites.

Once well established in a reptile collection, they can be very difficult to eradicate, as they move off the snake and even out of the vivarium to lay their eggs.

Pesticides that kill mites can also be harmful to reptiles and it is probably best to seek veterinary help in establishing a proper control programme. This will involve a treatment for the room that the snake is in, a different treatment for the vivarium itself and a third one to apply to the snake.

INTERNAL PARASITES

Most wild-caught snakes will harbour internal parasites. In the wild, the snake will live in balance with its parasitic burden but in captivity this may not be the case.

The stress of capture, transport round the world and subsequent sale will lower the snake's resistance and the parasites may increase in numbers, leading to disease.

In the case of worms with a direct life cycle, the vivarium will become contaminated with microscopic eggs that readily get back into the host snake and grow into more worms.

Any wild-caught or farmed snake should be checked for these unwanted guests. Any veterinary surgeon who regularly treats reptiles will be pleased to check a fresh faecal sample for you. If there are parasites present, it is important to get rid of them before they cause disease. Even if the results are negative, it can be a relief to know that you no longer need to worry about them.

VIRUSES

Modern research into diseases of snakes has started to reveal a collection of viruses that cause serious infections for which there is no specific treatment. Many infected snakes die. Others become carriers.

Some viruses cause mild disease in one species and fatal infections in another. This is a good reason for keeping snakes of different species in separate vivaria.

Infections may spread readily through a collection and, in some cases, have wiped out all the snakes on the premises.

Although there is no treatment, there are tests to see if a snake is already infected. While this may be of academic interest if you only have one snake, it can be very important information about new snakes that you are planning to

In some countries, such as the UK, the Grass Snake is legally protected, and requires special permission to be kept.

add to your own collection. Ask your vet for the most up-to-date information.

RESPIRATORY DISEASE

Snakes with respiratory disease may breathe with their mouths open. They are usually reluctant to feed and may have a discharge from the mouth. You may even notice them breathing more deeply or more quickly.

The entrance to the airway is on the floor of the mouth and you may be able to see discharge coming out if you carefully open the mouth and look.

Poor ventilation is a common cause of respiratory infections and, as well as seeking veterinary treatment, you will need to review the air quality in the vivarium.

▼ Macklot's Python.

BURNS

Thermal injuries happen when snakes come into contact with hot lighting or heating equipment. For some reason, they seem unable to appreciate the danger or pain, so they do not move away before damage is done.

Such injuries initially appear as reddish discolouration of the skin, but quickly progress to blisters, necrosis and sepsis. Deep burns must be very painful and may well be fatal.

Treatment needs to be intensive and prolonged. The injured area may retain the scars for the rest of the snake's life. Prevention is better than cure so make sure that heaters are protected by a wire cage and have a thermal cut-out which will activate if they overheat.

THIAMINE DEFICIENCY

This is a problem for fish-eaters.

Thiamine (Vitamin B1) is necessary for normal nerve function and is present in fresh fish in adequate amounts. But freezing lowers thiamine levels and increases the level of thiaminase, which is an enzyme that destroys the vitamin.

Prolonged feeding of thawed, frozen fish will lead to a deficiency.

Chihuahua Mountain King Snake.

Affected snakes at first twitch or 'star gaze' and eventually become paralysed. Treatment with thiamine injections is quick, cheap and very effective.

Boiling the frozen fish for a minute and then cooling it down before feeding it will destroy the thiaminase. Alternatively, supplement the frozen-fish diet with earthworms, tadpoles or fresh fish.

SWOLLEN EYES

Eyes may swell for a variety of reasons, but infections below the skin cap are a common cause.

The eyeball itself will no longer be visible and the eye may appear grey, yellow or blood-coloured. The surface of the eye may look dry and wrinkled.

Any attempt to touch the area may be vigorously resisted. For an animal that lacks a sense of hearing, eyesight is very important.

Most snakes' eyes are set on either side of the head, giving all-round vision. Going blind in one eye makes a snake vulnerable to events happening on the side that it can not see.

Prompt specialist surgery and antibiotic treatment will be needed if the snake's sight in the affected eye is to be saved.

During the shedding process, fluid forms between the old layer of skin and the new. This makes the eyes go a bluish colour a few days before shedding takes place.

Few snakes will feed at this time, perhaps because they cannot see what is to be eaten.

If the eyes remain bluish or swollen after a shed it may be because the cap over the eye does not come free when the rest of the skin is shed. These delicate structures are easily injured by ham-fisted interference. Do *not* try and remove the old skin cap with adhesive tape. If the snake does not appear in discomfort, and if it starts to eat again normally after the shed, it may be worth just waiting to see if two skin caps come away together at the next shed. If they do not, or if complications start to develop, it is time to get professional help from a vet experienced at treating reptiles.

NURSING CARE

Some principles of nursing care apply no matter what your snake is suffering from.

If the temperature is too low,

the snake's immune system will not work properly. Many reptile keepers raise the temperature in the vivarium to help an invalid fight an infection

Resistance to disease falls if the patient is not fed. If your snake is not eating voluntarily, ask your vet what you can do to provide nutritional support.

It is a natural instinct for most wild animals to hide if they are ill. This means that they are less obvious targets for predators who may be looking to attack weak specimens that will make an easy meal. Provide your snake with a small, upturned cardboard box with a hole in the side so that there is somewhere that he will feel safe. Dim the lighting to make your snake feel more hidden.

Even very tame snakes will prefer to be left alone when they are ill. Handle sick snakes as little as possible.

Guyanan Red Tail Boa: With careful management, your snake should live a long life and suffer few health problems.